DESIGN
Claire Leighton

TYPESETTING
Claire Leighton, Julie Smith

GRAPHICS
Julie Smith

PRODUCTION
Ruth Arthur
Sally Connolly
Neil Randles

DIRECTOR OF PRODUCTION
Gerald Hughes

CLB 3236
Published 1993 by
  Whitecap Books Ltd.
  1086 West 3rd Street
  North Vancouver, B.C.
  Canada V7P 3J6
©1993 Colour Library Books Ltd,
  Godalming, Surrey, England
Printed and bound in Hong Kong by Leefung Asco.
ISBN 1 55110 066 5

The Canadian Diary

WHITECAP
BOOKS

Every pine and fir and hemlock
Wore ermine too dear for an earl,
And the poorest twig on the elm-tree
Was ridged inch-deep with pearl.

James Russell Lowell
"The First Snow-Fall"

January

Winter in the Canadian Rockies

Birthstone: garnet

January

CAPRICORN
22 December – 20 January
Capricorns may experience hardship in early life but their resourcefulness makes them self-sufficient survivors. Often difficult to get to know, they are down-to-earth and highly responsible.

1
New Year's Day

1932 Birthday of Jackie Parker, football player

1966 The government permits colour TV in Canada

2

1908 The Royal Mint in Ottawa strikes its first coin

3

1939 Birthday of Bobby Hull, hockey star

4

1939 The world's first skating rink made of milk opens in Port Arthur, Ontario

5

Epiphany

6
Twelfth night

1827 Birthday of Sir Sandford Fleming, Canada's foremost railway engineer

7

Blowing snow near Dugald, Manitoba

January

Polarity: Capricorn is a negative or feminine sign. These signs have a self-repressive and passive tendency.

8

1945 Birthday of Dave Hodge, sports commentator

9

1802 Birthday of Catherine Parr Traill, author and pioneer

10

1935 Birthday of "Rompin' Ronnie" Hawkins, singer

11

1815 Birthday of Sir John A. Macdonald, first Canadian prime minister

12

1961 Terminal #1 opens at Toronto International Airport

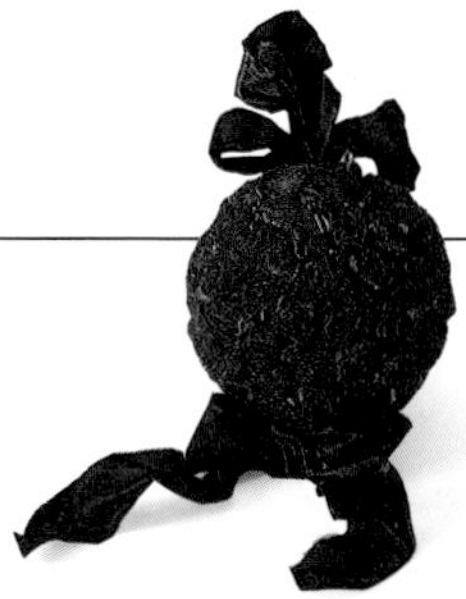

13

14

1855 Birthday of Homer Ransford Watson, painter

Hunter River, Prince Edward Island

January

Element: Capricorn is an earth sign. These signs are practical, realistic and restrained.

15

1949 RCAF officer J. Jolicoeur makes the first non-stop coast-to-coast flight, from Vancouver to Halifax

16

1965 The Canadian/American Auto Pact is signed in Austin Texas

17

18

1952 Birthday of Gilles Villeneuve, racing driver

1859 Birthday of Elizabeth Smith-Shortt, doctor and feminist revolutionary

19

1934 Birthday of Lloyd Robertson, broadcaster

20

21

1926 Birthday of Barry Broadfoot, journalist

Castle Mountain, Banff National Park

January

1908 Birthday of Sinclair Ross, novelist

22

23

24

25

26

1961 Birthday of Wayne Gretzky,
hockey star

27

1931 Birthday of Mordecai Richler,
author

28

1980 Canadian ambassador Ken Taylor
arranges the escape of six Americans
from Iran

Winter in rural Ontario

January

29

30

31

January 11, 1815, marks the birth of **Sir John A. Macdonald,** Canada's first Prime Minister. The major architect of the British North America Act, which created the confederation, he lived to see Canada's dominion extend from sea to sea.

Born in Scotland, Macdonald's family settled in Kingston, Ontario (then Upper Canada) in 1820. A lawyer and businessman, he was elected to the legislature in 1844 and quickly established himself as leader of the Conservative Party. By the 1860s it was clear that a coalition of British colonies in North America was necessary and Macdonald became its leading advocate; in 1867, he became the first prime minister of the new confederation. Macdonald continued to dominate Canadian politics until the election of 1891, which was won at the expense of his life. After a difficult winter campaign, he died on June 6, 1891.

Cape Tryon, Prince Edward Island

*Though we travel the world over
to find the beautiful, we must
carry it with us or we find it not.*

Ralph Waldo Emerson
"Essay on Art"

February

Lake Louise, Victoria Glacier, Alberta

Birthstone: amethyst

February

Element: Aquarius is an air sign. Air signs are mentally active, rational and communicative.

1

1895 Birthday of Conn Smythe, sportsman

2

1914 Birthday of Eric Kierans, politician

3

4

1909 Birthday of Jack Shadbolt, artist
1916 Parliament buildings destroyed by fire

5

6

1948 Figure skater Barbara Ann Scott wins an Olympic gold medal at St. Moritz, Switzerland

7

1886 Birthday of John Basset, publisher

Douglas fir forest, Vancouver Island,
British Columbia

February

8

1879 Canadian engineer Sir Sandford Fleming proposes to divide the world into 24 time zones, establishing a prime meridian in the Pacific

9

1894 Birthday of "Billy" Bishop, World War 1 fighter ace

10

1841 Act of Union proclaimed, providing a single government and legislature for the province of Canada

11

1922 A team of Toronto doctors, led by Dr. Frederick Banting, discovers insulin

12

1915 Birthday of Lorne Greene, actor

13

1969 FLQ blows up the Montreal Stock Exchange
1947 Imperial Oil's big strike at Leduc initiates Alberta's oil industry

14

Saint Valentine's Day

Iceberg off the Newfoundland coast

February

PISCES
19 February – 19 March
Pisceans have a natural aptitude for acting and a boundless imagination. They are sympathetic and highly tolerant. Often religious or mystical, Pisceans are incurable romantics.

15

1965 Queen Elizabeth II officially proclaims the red and white maple-leaf banner as Canada's new flag

16

17

1968 Skier Nancy Greene wins gold and silver medals at the Olympic games in Grenoble, France

18

1916 Birthday of Jean Drapeau, former Mayor of Montreal

19

1984 Speed skater Gaetan Boucher wins two gold medals to go with a silver at the Sarajevo Olympics

20

1930 Cairine Reay Wilson becomes first woman senator in Canada
1942 Birthday of Phil Esposito, hockey star
1942 Birthday of Buffy Sainte-Marie, singer

21

1942 Birthday of Roderick Haig-Brown, author and naturalist

Spring break-up in the Gulf of St. Lawrence,
Quebec

February

Polarity: Pisces is a negative or feminine sign. These signs have a self-repressive and passive tendency.

22

1903 Birthday of Morley Callaghan, novelist

23

1909 Baddeck Bay, NS: J.A.D. McCurdy makes the first Canadian airplane flight in the *Silver Dart*

24

1932 Birthday of John Vernon, actor

25

1887 Birthday of General A.G.L. McNaughton, army commander in World War II

1903 Birthday of King Clancy, hockey executive

26

1930 Birthday of Allan King, film producer

27

28 / 29

1960 Anne Heggeveit wins Canada's first Olympic gold medal in alpine skiing at Squaw Valley, Idaho

Sunrise in Mount Seymour Provincial Park,
British Columbia

Forth in the pleasing Spring
Thy beauty walks, Thy tenderness and love.
Wide flush the fields; the softening air is balm;
Echo the mountains round; the forest smiles;
And every sense, and every heart, is joy.

James Thompson
"A Hymn of The Seasons"

March

Mountain meadows near Banff, Alberta

Birthstone: aquamarine or bloodstone

March

1

Saint David's Day

2

3

1847 Birthday of Alexander Graham Bell, Scottish/Canadian/American inventor
1927 Birthday of William Kurelek, painter

4

1949 Birthday of Carroll Baker, singer

1975 TV cameras record Parliament for the first time

5

1844 First isssue of the Toronto *Globe*

1982 Steve Podborski clinches the World Cup in men's downhill skiing

6

1940 Birthday of Ken Danby, painter

7

1951 Birthday of Diane Jones Konihowski, pentathlete

The Narrows in St. John's Harbour,
Newfoundland

March

Quadruplicity: Pisces is a mutable sign. These signs are changeable and supremely adaptable.

8

9

1955 The Niagara suspension bridge opens

10

1876 Alexander Graham Bell makes the world's first telephone call from Brantford, Ontario

11

1969 The last R.C.M.P. dog sled patrol leaves Old Crow in the Yukon

12

1821 Birthday of Sir John Abbott, Canada's third prime minister
1912 Birthday of Irving Layton, poet

13

1914 Birthday of W.O. Mitchell, author
1919 Unions in Western Canada form "One Big Union," declaring support for the Bolsheviks

14

1916 Birthday of Sammy Luftspring, boxer

The Fraser Valley, British Columbia

March

ARIES
20 March – 20 April
Arians are brave and courageous, often fiercely defending the underdog. Limitless, dynamic energy is a spur to an Arian's adventures. He or she will be full of generosity and loyalty.

15

16

17

Saint Patrick's Day

18

19

Saint Joseph's Day

1885 Louis Riel and Metis followers seize a church at Batoche, Saskatchewan, starting their second rebellion

20

1939 Birthday of Brian Mulroney, 18th Canadian prime minister

21

Spring Equinox

1936 Birthday of Ed Broadbent, politician

La Martre, Quebec

March

1893 Montreal AAA wins the first Stanley Cup
1931 Birthday of William Shatner, actor

22

23

24

1936 Birthday of David Suzuki, naturalist

25

Lady Day

26

27

28

29

1778 Captain Cook lands at Nootka Sound

1867 The British North America Act was enacted, which established guidelines for confederation

30

31

1928 Birthday of Gordie Howe, hockey star

1949 Newfoundland becomes tenth province of Canada

Blue Rocks, Nova Scotia

Alexander Graham Bell was born on **March 3**, 1847, in Scotland and moved to Brantford, Ontario, with his parents in 1870. Ranked among the most important innovators of the nineteenth and twentieth centuries, Bell is probably best known for inventing the telephone. By the age of thirty-five, it had made him a rich man and he spent the rest of his life in scientific research and philanthropic work, involving himself in projects such as steam-powered aircraft, early atomic experiments, the photoelectric cell, the iron lung, desalination of seawater, the phonograph, gasoline-powered aircraft and hydrofoil boats. Bell had moved to Washington, D.C., to protect his business interests by 1882, but the family spent much time at their property at Baddeck, Nova Scotia, which was the site in 1909 of Canada's first manned flight.

We are what suns and winds and waters make us;
The mountains are our sponsors, and the rills
Fashion and win their nurseling with their smiles.
But where the land is dim from tyranny,
There tiny pleasures occupy the place

Walter Savage Landor
"Regeneration"

April

Mount Rundle, Vermilion Lake, Banff National Park

Birthstone: diamond

April

1

All-Fool's Day

2

1940 Birthday of Donald Jackson, figure skater
1975 CN Tower completed

3

1918 Birthday of Louis Applebaum, composer/conductor

4

1952 Birthday of Karen Magnussen, figure skater

5

1958 In the world's largest non-atomic explosion, engineers destroyed shipping hazard Ripple Rock off Campbell River, B.C.

6

1886 City of Vancouver incorporated

7

1908 Birthday of Percy Faith, conductor

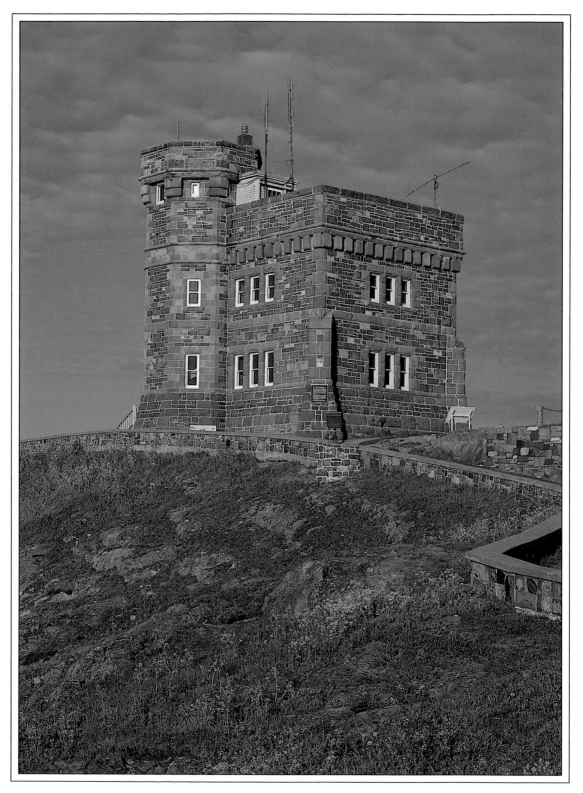

The Cabot Tower, St. John's, Newfoundland

April

1883 Birthday of Mary Pickford, actress

8

1931 Birthday of Richard Hatfield, New Brunswick politician

9

1937 Trans-Canada Airlines created by Act of Parliament

10

1914 Birthday of Robert Stanfield, politician

11

12

1825 Birthday of Thomas D'Arcy McGee, father of Confederation

13

1932 Birthday of Bill Bennett, British Columbia politician

14

Spring colour near Springbrook,
Prince Edward Island

April

Each zodiac sign corresponds to a part of the body. **Aries** corresponds to the head as a whole.

15

1861 Birthday of Bliss Carman, poet

16

1908 Birthday of J. Armand Bombardier, inventor of the snowmobile

17

1982 Canadian Constitution effected

18

19

1900 Jim Cafferty, Bill Sherring and Frank Hughson, the first Canadians to run the Boston Marathon, finish first, second and third

20

1950 Birthday of Toller Cranston, figure skater

1989 Last printing of Canadian $1 bills

21

1926 Birthday of Queen Elizabeth II

Spring thunder storm in rural Ontario

April

TAURUS
21 April – 21 May
Taureans are seekers of peace and stability. Unambitious, they are quite happy to be the powerhouse behind the scenes. They are sensible and healthily cynical, but also possess a gentle facet.

22

23
Saint George's Day

1897 Birthday of Lester B. Pearson, 14th Canadian prime minister

24

1933 Birthday of Alan Eagleson, sports agent

25
Saint Mark's Day

1849 Tories, enraged over the Rebellion Losses Bill, sack and burn the Parliament in Montreal

26

1869 Ottawa's noon day gun fired for the first time

27

28

1967 Expo opens in Montreal

Blossoms and dandelions in the Okanagan
Valley, British Columbia

April

Polarity: Taurus is a negative or feminine sign. These signs have a self-repressive and passive tendency.

29

1903 A landslide at Frank, Alberta kills 70 of the community's 600 people

30

1623 Birthday of François de Laval, first Bishop of Quebec

The CN Tower in Toronto, completed **April 2,** 1975, still holds the record as the tallest free-standing structure in the world. Built at a cost of $52 million, the hexagonal concrete tower is braced by three tapering wings that rise to 330 metres. The tower rises another 120 metres and is topped by a 100-metre steel mast giving a total height of 553 metres.

Glass-walled elevators take thousands of visitors each year to the 342 metre level, where there is a skypod featuring observation decks and the world's highest revolving restaurant. The communications antenna atop the tower transmits both broadcast and microwave signals.

Long Beach, Vancouver Island,
British Columbia

Spring came with tiny lances thrusting,
And earth was clad in peeping green;
In russet bark, the twigs incrusting,
Tenderest blossom-points were seen;
A robin courier proclaimed good cheer:
Summer will soon arrive, for I am here.

Wilbur Larremore
"Blossom Time"

May

Early morning over Okanagan Lake, British Columbia

Birthstone: emerald

May

Element: Taurus is an earth sign. These signs are practical, realistic and restrained.

1

1831 Birthday of Emily Stowe, first woman doctor in Canada

2

1670 Hudson's Bay Company chartered, making it the oldest incorporated joint-stock merchandising company in the English-speaking world

1939 National Film Board established

1986 Expo opens in Vancouver

3

4

1928 Birthday of Maynard Ferguson, jazz trumpet player

5

6

7

1894 Birthday of George Drew, politician

Canola crop in southern Alberta

May

Quadruplicity: Taurus is a fixed sign. These signs are steadfast sustainers.

8

1912 Birthday of George Woodcock, author

9

1929 Birthday of Barbara Ann Scott, figure skater

10

1929 Birthday of Peter Newman, journalist

11

1943 Birthday of Nancy Greene, skier

12

1885 Canadian Militia defeat the Metis at Batoche, ending the North-West rebellion
1921 Birthday of Farley Mowat, author

13

14

1904 Etienne Desmarteau wins Canada's first Olympic gold medal–throwing the hammer in St. Louis

Aspens in spring, Banff National Park,
Alberta

May

Taurus is the second sign of the zodiac and its symbol is the bull. This sign corresponds to the throat and neck of the human anatomy.

1919 Onset of Winnipeg General Strike

15

16

17

1806 Birthday of Dr. George B. Chisholm, psychiatrist

18

1908 Birthday of Percy Williams, Olympic sprinter

19

1948 Birthday of Bobby Orr, Hockey star

20

1917 Birthday of actor Raymond Burr, famous for his television role as Perry Mason

21

Percé Rock, Quebec

May

22

1987 Wheelchair athlete Rick Hansen completes his around-the-world tour in Vancouver

23

1873 North-West Mounted Police formed

24

1918 Canadian women get the federal vote
1930 Birthday of Robert Bateman, artist
1934 Birthday of Annette, Emilie, Yvonne, Cecile and Marie: the Dionne quintuplets

25

Victoria Day

1879 Birthday of William Maxwell Aitken (Lord Beaverbrook), industrialist and press baron

26

1919 Birthday of Canadian actor Jay Silverheels, who played Tonto in television's Lone Ranger series

27

28

1902 Toronto physicist Ernest Rutherford announces his discovery of particles smaller than atoms

Niagara Falls, Ontario

May

29

1904 Birthday of Eugene Forsey, senator and constitutional expert

30

31

1866 Fenians invade Canada

Canada's national police force had its birth on **May 23,** 1873, when the **North-West Mounted Police** was created by an Act of Parliament. By the next year 300 recruits wearing the trademark scarlet tunic and blue trousers were sent to winter in Fort Garry. This small force was charged with the formidable duty of administering justice in the vast hinterlands of the west, a territory occupied by natives made restless by the disruption of their traditional ways, hard-pressed settlers, and American whiskey-traders.

By the end of the next decade a network of posts dotted the territories. The suppression of the whiskey trade, and the fairness and tact of the force, won the respect of natives and helped in the transition of the west. In 1920 the force was renamed the Royal Canadian Mounted Police and given national jurisdiction with headquarters in Ottawa.

Farm near Newmarket, Ontario

When from our better selves we have too long
Been parted by the hurrying world, and droop,
Sick of its business, of its pleasures tired,
How gracious, how benign, is solitude.

William Wordsworth
"The Prelude"

June

Maligne Lake, Jasper National Park

Birthstone: agate, pearl, moonstone or alexandrite

June

1

2

1877 A handful of North-West Mounted Police meet Chief Sitting Bull and 5,000 fugitive Indians at Whitmud Creek. The Sioux are given sanctuary in Canada

3

1989 Toronto's Sky Dome is officially opened

4

5

1939 Birthday of Joe Clark, politician

6

1944 D-Day: Canadians invade Normandy

7

1929 Birthday of John Turner, politician

Salt Water Marsh, near St. Ann's Cape Breton
Island, Nova Scota

June

1928 Birthday of John Labatt, brewer

8

1961 Birthday of Michael J. Fox, film actor

9

1791 Constitutional Act divides Upper Canada from Lower Canada

10

1920 Birthday of Tom Patterson, founder of the Stratford Shakespearean Festival

11

1915 Birthday of Earl Cameron, newscaster

12

13

1924 Birthday of Arthur Erickson, architect
1933 Birthday of Robert Bourassa, Quebec politician

14

Totems, Queen Charlotte Islands,
British Columbia

June

15

World Children's Day

1846 The Oregon Boundary Treaty sets the 49th parallel as the border between Western Canada and the USA

16

17

1881 Birthday of Tommy Burns, the only Canadain boxer to capture the world heavyweight title

18

1812 USA declares war on Britain, and invades Canada

19

1903 Birthday of Guy Lombardo, band leader
1983 B.C. Place Stadium opens in Vancouver

20

1945 Birthday of Anne Murray, singer and musician

21

1844 Russian surveyor Zagoskin becomes the first European to map the Yukon
1957 Ellen Fairclough becomes Canada's first female cabinet minister

Blind River, Ontario

June

CANCER
22 June – 22 July
Cancers value their security, enjoying the safety and comfort of the familiar. They are emotionally vulnerable and so take steps to protect themselves. They make excellent conciliators.

22

1812 Laura Secord walks 30 km from Queenston to Beaver Dams to warn of an impending American attack

23

1887 Banff becomes Canada's first national park

1985 An Air India jet en route from Toronto explodes off Ireland killing 329, including 280 Canadians

Midsummer

24

Saint John the Baptist's Day

1497 John Cabot lands on Canadian soil

1611 Mutiny on the *Discovery* —Henry Hudson set adrift

1866 Georges Belcourt takes the first Canadian ride in an automobile

25

1917 Birthday of "Whipper Billy" Watson, wrestler

26

27

1854 Canadian chemist Abraham Gesner patents kerosene

1936 Birthday of Russ Jackson, football player

28

29

Saint Peter's Day

30

On **June 24,** 1457, **John Cabot** landed on the North American continent, the first recorded landfall since the Norse.

Of Italian birth, Cabot moved to England in 1484 and sailed for King Henry VII. Leaving from Bristol on May 2, 1497 with eighteen men, he landed on what was probably Cape Breton Island and claimed the land for England. In 1498 he undertook a second, much larger expedition. He explored Greenland and travelled south to 38 degrees North latitude, but as supplies ran low and he found no trace of the eastern civilization he sought, he returned home. It is thought that he died on the homeward voyage, although some of his ships returned to Bristol, earning Cabot recognition as the explorer who "discovered" North America and establishing a British claim to the new lands.

Sunset near Regina, Saskatchewan

How blest beyond all blessings are farmers,
if they but knew their happiness!
Far from the clash of arms, the most just
earth brings forth from the soil an easy living.

Virgil
"Georgics II"

July

Rural scene near St. Williams, Ontario

Birthstone: ruby

July

Element: Cancer is a water sign. These signs are artistic, emotional and perceptive.

1

Canada Day

1867 Dominion of Canada created

1873 Prince Edward Island enters confederation

1935 Hundereds of striking workers from Western Canada end their "On to Ottawa Trek" by rioting in Regina

2

3

Saint Thomas's Day

1608 City of Quebec founded

1934 Establishment of the Bank of Canada

4

1816 Birthday of Hiram Walker, distiller

5

6

1930 Birthday of George "Chief" Armstrong, hockey player and coach

7

1905 Birthday of Clarence Campbell, former president of the National Hockey League

The Big Flower Pot, Georgian Bay National
Park, Ontario

July

8

9

10

1931 Birthday of Alice Munro, author

11

1950 Birthday of Liona Boyd, guitarist

12

1920 Birthday of Pierre Berton, author
1930 Birthday of Gordon Pinsent, actor/writer

13

14

1912 Birthday of Northrop Frye, literary scholar

Alpine flowers, Manning Park,
British Columbia

July

Cancer is the fourth sign of the zodiac and its symbol is the crab. This sign corresponds to the breasts and the stomach of the human anatomy.

15

Saint Swithin's Day

1774 Juan Perez Hernandez becomes first European to contact Northwest Coast Indians
1870 Manitoba becomes Canada's fifth province

16

1917 Artist Tom Thompson's body is found in Canoe Lake, Ontario

17

1771 Samuel Hearne becomes first European to sight the north coast of North America
1934 Birthday of Donald Sutherland, actor

18

1926 Birthday of Margaret Laurence, author
1911 Birthday of Hume Cronyn, actor

19

20

1871 British Columbia joins Confederation

21

1836 Opening of the Champlain and Saint Lawrence Railroad, the first in Canada
1911 Birthday of Marshall McLuhan, intellectual

Field of rye, Saskatchewan

July

22

1793 Alexander Mackenzie becomes the first explorer to cross North America by land
1968 Fire destroys Winnipeg's St. Boniface Basilica

23

1860 Prince Edward Albert makes the first official royal visit to Canada

24

1899 Birthday of Chief Dan George
1534 Jacques Cartier claims the Gaspé for France
1967 French President Charles de Gaulle cries "Vive le Quebec libre!" from the balcony of Montreal's city hall

25

1931 Birthday of Maureen Forrester, opera singer

Saint James's Day

26

27

28

1786 John Molson sets up his brewery in Montreal
1958 Birthday of Terry Fox, Marathon of Hope runner

Citadel Pass, British Columbia

July

29

1941 Birthday of Lloyd Bochner, actor

1938 Birthday of Peter Jennings, newscaster

30

1924 Birthday of Paul Anka, singer
1962 Trans-Canada Highway, the longest national highway in the world, opens at Rogers Pass, B.C.

31

Terry Fox was born in Winnipeg on **July 28,** 1958. In his short life he became a national hero, demonstrating tremendous courage and creating a fund that continues to contribute millions of dollars annually to cancer research. Diagnosed in 1977 with a rare bone cancer, osteogenic sarcoma, Fox underwent surgery to amputate most of one leg. He conceived the idea of a cross-Canada run to generate money for cancer research after the surgery.

The run began in St. John's, Newfoundland, on April 12, 1980. It ended on September 1 in Thunder Bay, when the cancer that had spread to his lungs made it impossible to continue. He had covered 5373 kilometres, averaging nearly 40 kilometres a day, and raised $ 1.7 million, later augmented by another $ 23 million.

Mount Robson Provincial Park,
British Columbia

Calm was the day, and through the trembling air
Sweet breathing Zephyrus did softly play,
A gentle spirit, that lightly did delay
Hot Titan's beams, which then did glister fair

Edmund Spenser
"Prothalmion"

August

Tofino Harbour on Vancouver Island

Birthstone: peridot or sardonyx

August

Element: Leo is a fire sign. These signs are enthusiastic, energetic and assertive.

1

1834 Slavery abolished in all British Colonies–meaning freedom for the approximately 50 in British North America

2

1862 Birthday of Duncan Campbell Scott, poet and writer

3

4

1900 Birthday of Elizabeth, the Queen Mother
1914 Canada enters the First World War

5

1918 Birthday of Betty Oliphant, ballet mistress

6

1820 Birthday of Sir Donald Smith (Lord Strathcona), politician and financier

7

Emerald Lake, Yoho National Park,
British Columbia

August

8

1947 Birthday of Ken Dryden, hockey goalkeeper and writer

9

10

1792 Paper money introduced by the Canada Banking Company

1876 The world's first long distance telephone call is conducted by Alexander Graham Bell and Thomas Watson between Brantford and Paris, Ontario

11

12

13

1535 Jacques Cartier misinterprets the Huron word for village, and names the nation "Canada"

1949 Birthday of Bobby Clarke, hockey player and coach

14

1803 Birthday of Sir James Douglas, "Father of British Columbia"

Algonquin Provincial Park, Ontario

August

15

1890 Canada's first electric streetcars run in Toronto

1925 Birthday of Oscar Peterson, concert jazz pianist

16

1812 Major-General Isaac Brock captures Detroit

1896 Gold discovered in the Klondike River, Yukon

17

18

1893 Birthday of Sir Ernest MacMillan, conductor/composer

19

1794 Captain George Vancouver concludes that a Northwest Passage from the West Coast does not exist

1942 Dieppe: Canadians make a disastrous raid, losing 900 soldiers in nine hours

20

1949 The biggest earthquake recorded in Canada hits the West Coast

21

Reed Lake, Manitoba

August

VIRGO
24 August – 23 September
Virgos value knowledge highly. They make good teachers and advisers, while avoiding positions of prominent power. Often shy, Virgos hide their sensitivity under a self-controlled surface.

22

23

1920 Birthday of Alex Colville, painter

24
Saint Bartholomew's Day

1785 First issue of the *Montreal Gazette*

1944 Birthday of Conrad Black, business executive

25

1957 Birthday of Rick Hanson, athlete

26

27

28

1913 Birthday of Robertson Davies, author

Parliament Building, Victoria,
British Columbia

August

Polarity: Virgo is a negative or feminine sign. These signs have a self-repressive and passive tendecy.

29

30

31

1931 Birthday of Jean Beliveau, hockey player

Canadian and British soldiers joined together on **August 19**, 1942, in a bloody battle on the northwest coast of France. Designed to test the strength of Hitler's coastal defence on the continent and provide strategic information for future amphibious attacks, the raid on Dieppe took a high toll on lives and equipment.

In the nine hours it lasted, the raid claimed the lives of more than 900 of the 5000 Canadian soldiers deployed and saw a further 1874 taken prisoner. Two Canadians received the Victoria Cross: Hon. Capt. J.W. Foote, of the Royal Hamilton Light Infantry and Lt. Col. C.C. Merritt, commanding officer of the South Saskatchewan Regiment. The Allies lost 106 aircraft and 81 airmen, the RCAF 13 planes and 10 pilots. Despite the heavy losses, valuable information was gained for future raids in North Africa, Italy and Normandy.

A maple's russet hues heralds the approach
of autumn

Ah, sunflower! weary of time,
Who countest the steps of the sun;
Seeking after that sweet golden clime
Where the traveller's journey is done

William Blake
"Ah! Sunflower"

September

Sunflower fields in southern Manitoba

Birthstone: sapphire

September

1

1905 Saskatchewan and Alberta join Confederation
1923 Birthday of Lord Thompson of Fleet, newspaper magnate

2

1912 The first Calgary Stampede, or "The Last and Best Great West Frontier Days Celebration," opens

3

4

5

1953 Birthday of Dave Murray, downhill skier

6

1979 Canada's first gold bullion coin sold

7

1925 Birthday of Allan Blakeney, Saskatchewan politician

The prairies near Antelope, Saskatchewan

September

Quadruplicity: Virgo is a mutable sign. These signs are changeable and supremely adaptable.

8

1952 Canada's first TV station, CBC's CBFT, begins broadcasting

9

1954 Marilyn Bell becomes the first to swim across Lake Ontario

10

1904 Bill Miner and his gang rob the CPR near Vancouver
1939 Canada enters the Second World War

11

1920 Birthday of Dalton Camp, journalist and politician

12

1937 Birthday of George Chuvalo, heavyweight boxer
1943 Birthday of Michael Ondaatje, author and poet

13

1759 General Montcalm loses to General Wolfe in the Battle of the Plains of Abraham, Quebec

14

A solitary oak dominates this desolate grassland scene

September

Virgo is the sixth sign of the zodiac and its symbol is the virgin. The sign corresponds to the abdomen and intestines of the human anatomy.

15

1901 Birthday of Gweneth Lloyd, ballet choreographer

16

17

18

1895 Birthday of John Diefenbaker, 13th prime minister of Canada

1933 Birthday of Scotty Bowman, hockey executive

19

1875 The Supreme Court of Canada created

1889 A massive rockslide in Quebec City buries Champlain Street

20

1951 Birthday of Guy Lafleur, hockey player

21

1902 Birthday of Howie Morenz, hockey player

1934 Birthday of Leonard Cohen, musician and author

Saint Matthew's Day

The Old Mill, King Landing Historical
Settlement, New Brunswick

September

LIBRA
24 September – 23 October
Librans are seekers after perfection and harmony, passionately believing in fairness and equality. Their chief skill lies in the field of diplomacy. Librans are full of charm and style.

22

Fall Equinox

1897 Birthday of Walter Pidgeon, actor

23

24

1932 Birthday of Glenn Gould, concert pianist

25

1827 Cornerstone of the Rideau Canal laid

26

1988 Sprinter Ben Johnson is stripped of his gold medal in Seoul, Korea after testing positive to illegal drugs

27

28

1962 Alouette I, Canada's first orbiting satellite is launched into space

29

Michaelmas

30

One of the pivotal battles in Canadian history occurred on the **Plains of Abraham** on **September 13, 1759.**

That day Maj.-General James Wolfe, who had sailed up the St. Lawence River at the head of a powerful British force, landed and climbed the cliffs above Quebec, intent on capturing the fortress for the British. A flustered Lt.General Marquis de Montcalm led his French militia into battle, where they were met by British infantry fire.

Both Wolfe and Montcalm were mortally injured in the battle that ensued. That night the French retreated farther up the St. Lawrence, leaving Quebec to surrender five days later. An attempt to recover the city in 1760 failed, and New France fell later that year with the British capture of Montreal.

The first change of colour in Ontario

It is the hour when life's constraint
A moment's ease is given;
When earth is like a holy saint,
Stilled, sanctified and shriven,
And the deep-breathing heart grows faint
To be so near to heaven.

Grace Ellery Channing-Stetson
"A Song of Arno"

October

Sunset on Otter Lake, Ontario

Birthstone: opal or pink tourmaline

October

Element: Libra is an air sign. Air signs are mentally active, rational and communicative.

1

1578 Martin Frobisher returns to England after his third trip to Canada with 1,000 tons of useless ore

2

1988 Boxer Lennox Lewis wins Canadian gold in the Olyimpic heavyweight division in Seoul, Korea

3

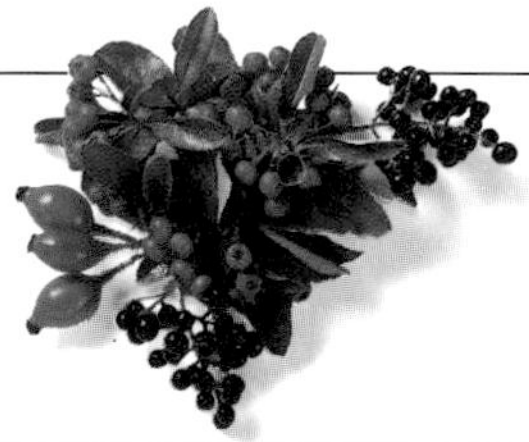

4

1909 Birthday of John D. Eaton, financier

5

1984 Marc Garneau becomes first Canadian to visit outer space

6

1843 Montreal declared the capital of Canada

7

1763 The Royal Proclamation defines the boundaries of Quebec

Fall in Muskoka, Ontario

October

Quadruplicity: Libra is a cardinal sign. These signs are enterprising instigators.

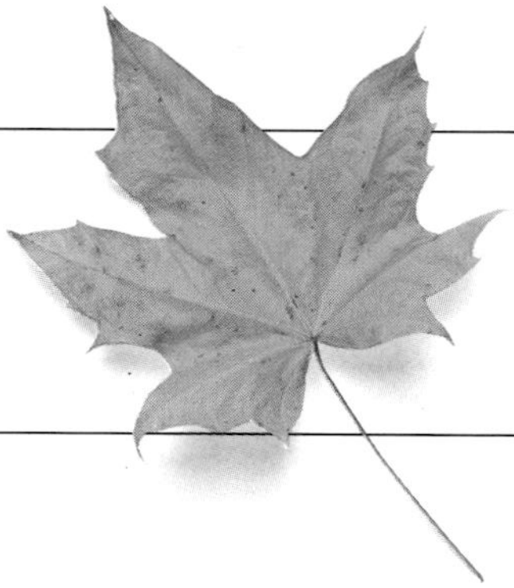

8

9

10

1678 The Brandy Parliament of New France decides to ignore the missionaries and keep selling liquor to the Indians

11

1899 Canada joins the Boer War

12

1909 Birthday of Dorothy Livesay, poet

13

1812 General Isaac Brock is shot and killed at the battle of Queenston Heights while leading an attack against American forces

14

1763 Birthday of John Molson, banker and brewer

Lake Superior and Nipigon Bay, Ontario

October

15

1908 Birthday of John Kenneth Galbraith, economist

16

1970 October crisis: Canada enters a state of "apprehended insurrection" under the War Measures Act

17

1760 The British raze Louisbourg, Cape Breton

18

Saint Luke's Day

1919 Birthday of Pierre Eliott Trudeau, 15th Canadian prime minister

19

1939 Birthday of Tommy Ambrose, country singer

20

1873 Birthday of Nellie McClung, novelist and suffragist

21

Aerial view near Manitoulin Island, Ontario

October

1844 Birthday of Louis Riel, revolutionary

22

1980 *The Globe and Mail* becomes the nation's first newspaper to employ satellite technology

23

1929 Birthday of Hubert Aquin, novelist

24

United Nations Day

25

26

1977 Canada's longest kidnapping ends when credit union manager Charles Marion is released after 83 days in captivity, in Quebec

27

1938 Birthday of Gary Cowan, golfer

28

Cape Breton Highlands National Park,
Nova Scotia

October

Polarity: Scorpio is a negative or feminine sign. These signs have a self-repressive and passive tendency.

29

30

31

Hallowe'en

Born at the Red River Settlement in Manitoba on **October 22,** 1844, **Louis Riel** became one of the most controversial figures in Canadian political life. Over one hundred years after his death, there is still debate over his role and the punishment meted out by the government. Riel led two popular revolts against the federal government. The Red River Rebellion of 1870 ensured bilingual services in the new province of Manitoba and saw 1,400,000 acres granted to the Metis. Some years later, Saskatchewan Metis asked Riel to help establish their legal rights, but a more powerful federal government, aided by the newly established North-West Mounted Police, quelled the armed rebellion at Batoche. Riel was tried for treason and executed on November 16, 1885.

Moonrise near Moose Jaw, Saskatchewan

Where ancient forests round us spread,
Where bends the cataract's ocean fall,
On the lone mountain's silent head,
There are thy temples, God of all!

Andrews Norton
"Hymn For The Dedication of a Church"

November

Peyto Lake, Banff National Park

Birthstone: topaz or citrine

November

Element: Scorpio is a water sign. These signs are artistic, emotional and peceptive

1

All Saints' Day

1949 Birthday of David Foster, composer and musical arranger

2

1869 Metis forces under Louis Riel seize Ft. Garry, bringing about their first rebellion

3

1873 Opening of the Bank of Montreal, Canada's first bank

4

1838 Martial law proclaimed in Lower Canada to quell the *patriote* rebellion

5

Guy Fawke's Day

1959 Birthday of Bryan Adams, musician and singer

6

7

1885 Driving of the "Last Spike" of the CPR, Canada's first transcontinental railway, in Eagle Pass, B.C.
1943 Birthday of Joni Mitchell, singer and musician

Morning mist over grassland near Erickson,
Manitoba

November

Quadruplicity: Scorpio is a fixed sign. These signs are steadfast sustainers.

8

1881 Birthday of Clarence Gagnon, painter

9

10

11

1918 Armistice Day: World War I ends, with Canadians having reached the town of Mons, Belgium

Remembrance Day

12

1945 Birthday of Neil Young, singer
1951 First performance of the National Ballet of Canada

13

1874 The Ku Klux Klan conduct the first train robbery in Canada, taking $45,000 from the Great Western Railway near Toronto

14

1606 Acadian settlers perform *Theatre de Neptune,* the first drama in the New World

Howe Sound, British Columbia

November

15

16

1945 Birthday of Martine Van Hamel, ballerina

17

1938 The Lion's Gate Bridge, linking Vancouver to the North Shore, is officially opened

18

1939 Birthday of Margaret Atwood, author
1929 Tidal wave hits Newfoundland's Birin Peninsula
1961 Saskatchewan becomes first province covered by medicare

19

1869 The Hudson's Bay Company transfers Rupert's Land to the Crown

20

1841 Birthday of Sir Wilfrid Laurier, 7th prime minister of Canada

21

1919 Golden Boy statue erected over Manitoba's legislature buildings
1921 King George grants Canada a coat of arms

The Coast Mountains near Bella Coola,
British Columbia

November

SAGITTARIUS
23 November – 21 December
Sagittarians adore excitement and adventure. Bold and impulsive, they are natural explorers thriving on change and constant mental stimulation. Sagittarians are often trend-setters.

22

23

1837 Patriots repulse government forces at St. Denis, in the Lower Canada Rebellion

1937 *The Governor General's Literary Awards* are established by the Canadian Authors' Association

24

25

1917 Establishment in Montreal of the National Hockey League
1938 Birthday of Rich Little, impressionist

26

27

1956 Canada grants free passage to refugees from the Hungarian revolution

28

1829 Completion of the Welland Canal

29

1840 Birthday of Henry Birks, silversmith
1874 Birthday of Lucy Maud Montgomery, novelist

30

Saint Andrew's Day

Construction of the transcontinental **Canadian Pacific Railway** was an amazing physical achievement. The line pushed through rock, muskeg, and some of the most daunting mountain terrain ever spanned, but the railway also represented the challenge of binding the distant provinces of Canada into a cohesive nation.

British Columbia entered Confederation on condition that a transcontinental railway link be completed. At the beginning of **November,** 1885, with only a few rails yet to be laid, Engine 148, towing railcars "Tepedia" and "Saskatchewan" with Canadian Pacific Railway officials and directors aboard, started the first transcontinental trek. A week later, at Craigellachie, in the Gold Range, the small group watched **Donald A. Smith** ceremonially drive home the last iron spike linking the eastern and western sections of railway.

The Richardson Mountains, Yukon

In that land all is and nothing's ought;
No owners or notices, only birds;
No walls anywhere, only lean wire of words
Worming brokenly out from eaten thought

William Robert Rogers
"Neither Here Nor There"

December

Mount Edith Cavell, Jasper National Park

Birthstone: turquoise or zircon

December

1

1899 The world's longest covered bridge is opened in Hartland, New Brunswick

2

1989 Audrey McLaughlin becomes the first woman to lead a national political party

3

1960 Annette Toft, Canada's 2,000,000th immigrant since 1945, arrives from Denmark

4

5

1837 William Lyon Mackenzie leads the Yonge Street Rebellion in Toronto, demanding responsible government

6

1917 A French munitions ship explodes in Halifax Harbour, leaving over 1,000 dead and 6,000 homeless

1989 Marc Lepine murders fourteen female students at the University of Montreal before committing suicide

7

1940 Birthday of Gerry Cheevers, hockey goalkeeper

The Coast Mountains, British Columbia

December

Quadruplicity: Sagittarius is a mutable sign. These signs are changeable and supremely adaptable.

8

9

1935 Birthday of Christoper Pratt, artist

10

11

1931 The Statute of Westminster grants all British colonies, including Canada, full legal freedom

12

1901 Marconi's first telegraph message is received from England at Signal Hill, St. John's, Newfoundland
1949 Nancy Hodges named Speaker of the B.C. legislature, the first woman speaker in the Commonwealth

13

1887 Toronto's *Saturday Night* magazine sells out its first issue of 9,500 copies
1939 Birthday of Christoper Plummer, actor

14

Lupine Falls, British Columbia

December

15

16

17

1874 Birthday of William Lyon Mackenzie King, Canada's 10th prime minister

1950 Canadian troops arrive in Korea

18

1846 Canada's first telegram sent, linking Toronto with Hamilton

19

1924 Birthday of Judy La Marsh, politician and journalist

20

1902 Guglielmo Marconi establishes permanent radio communication between Cape Breton and Great Britian

21

St. Mark's Parish Hall, Niagara-on-the-Lake,
Ontario

December

CAPRICORN
22 December – 20 January
Capricorns may experience hardship in
early life but their resourcefulness
makes them self-sufficient survivors.
Often difficult to get to know, they are
down-to-earth and highly responsible.

22

23

1908 Birthday of Yousuf Karsh,
photographer

1983 Jeanne Sauvé becomes the first
woman to be appointed Governor
General of Canada

24

Christmas Eve

1900 Birthday of Joseph Smallwood,
Newfoundland politician

25

Christmas Day

26

Boxing Day

27

1913 Birthday of Ian D. Sinclair,
industrialist

28

1929 Birthday of Terry Sawchuck,
hockey goalkeeper

Winter in the Hunter River Valley,
Prince Edward Island

December

29

30

1869 Birthday of Stephen Leacock, author and humourist
1942 Birthday of Matt Cohen, author

31

1857 Queen Victoria chooses Ottawa as the new capital of Canada
1883 Birthday of Lester Patrick, hockey executive

New Year's Eve

Although he was a political economist, essayist and historian, **Stephen Leacock's** name has become synonymous with humour, and a particularly Canadian humour.
He was born in England on **December 30,** 1869, and grew up on a farm near Lake Simcoe, Ontario. He studied economics and political science at the universities of Montreal and Chicago, then taught at McGill until his retirement in 1936. He was a prolific writer, and his humorous pieces and essays on social issues, politics, economics, education, geography, history and literary criticism appeared in numerous magazines.
Leacock is probably best known for *Sunshine Sketches of a Little Town*, in which he takes a fond and slightly quizzical look at the fictional Canadian town of Mariposa.

Winter sunset in Birds Hill Provincial Park,
Manitoba

Lake Nicola, British Columbia

PICTURE CREDITS
Gordon Fisher/First Light: Nov 15
John Glover: Title page
Chris Harris/First Light: July 29
Richard Hartmier/First Light: Nov 22
Thomas Kitchen/First Light: Feb 1, April 8, May 1, May 15, Oct 15
Alan Marsh/First Light: Jan 22
Dave Reede/First Light: Jan 1, June 22, Sept 8, Nov opener, Dec 29
Steve Shortt/First Light: July 22, Dec 8
Donald Standfield/First Light: Aug 29, Sept 22
Ken Straiton/First Light: April 15, Sept 15
John Sylvester/First Light: Jan 8, 29, Feb 15, Mar 1, Dec 22
Jürgen Vogt: Mar 15, 22, May 22, 29, June 15, July 15, Aug 15,
Sept opener, Sept 1, Oct 1, 29
Ron Watts/First Light: Feb 8, Aug 8
Wayne Wegner/First Light: July 1
Dale Wilson/First Light: April 1, June 1, Oct 22

All other photographs: Michael Burch

Lake Maligne and Spirit Island, Jasper
National Park, Alberta